AF207014

FOCUS ON ARTIFICIAL INTELLIGENCE

ARTIFICIAL INTELLIGENCE AND THE CHANGING JOB MARKET

by George Anthony Kulz

BrightPoint Press

San Diego, CA

© 2025 BrightPoint Press
an imprint of ReferencePoint Press, Inc.
Printed in the United States

For more information, contact:
BrightPoint Press
PO Box 27779
San Diego, CA 92198
www.BrightPointPress.com

LIBRARY OF CONGRESS CATALOGING-IN-PUBLICATION DATA

Name: Kulz, George Anthony, author.
Title: Artificial Intelligence and the Changing Job Market / by George Anthony Kulz.
Description: San Diego, CA: BrightPoint Press, Inc., 2025 | Series: Focus on Artificial
  Intelligence | Audience: Grade 7 to 9 | Includes biblio graphical references and index.
Identifiers: ISBN: 9781678209483 (hardcover) | ISBN: 9781678209490 (eBook)
The complete Library of Congress record is available at www.loc.gov.

CONTENTS

AT A GLANCE — 4

INTRODUCTION — 6
THE HOTEL OF THE FUTURE

CHAPTER ONE — 12
WHAT IS ARTIFICIAL INTELLIGENCE?

CHAPTER TWO — 22
AI IN THE WORKPLACE

CHAPTER THREE — 34
FUTURE OF AI IN THE WORKPLACE

CHAPTER FOUR — 46
CONCERNS ABOUT AI IN THE WORKPLACE

Glossary — 58
Source Notes — 59
For Further Research — 60
Index — 62
Image Credits — 63
About the Author — 64

AT A GLANCE

- Artificial intelligence (AI) is the ability of a computer to perform tasks usually done by humans and to learn from experience.

- Alan Turing was a pioneer in the field of computers. In the 1950s he wrote about the future possibilities of AI.

- In a 2022 survey, 62 percent of Americans felt AI would have a major impact on workers.

- Autonomous vehicles are projected to cause the loss of millions of jobs, but technical jobs are estimated to grow.

- Generative AI identifies patterns by studying large amounts of data. It then creates something new based on what it learned from those patterns.

- In a 2023 survey, 49 percent of businesses surveyed reported using ChatGPT and 48 percent of those businesses have replaced workers with ChatGPT.

- Knowing the strengths and weaknesses of AI will help companies find the smartest ways to use it for their business. Training and testing of AI will also be beneficial.

- In 2022, President Biden proposed an AI Bill of Rights, designed to protect humans' rights in the future.

THE HOTEL OF THE FUTURE

At the Waldorf Hotel, the hotel manager greets a guest at the door. "Good evening. Do you have a reservation?"

"Yes," the guest responds.

"Excellent," the manager says. "Please check in at the front desk."

The guest walks up to the desk.

"Please tell me your name," a voice speaks from the desk. The guest responds with her name. "I see you have a room with

In the future, robots will likely handle tasks such as checking in hotel guests and transporting luggage to rooms.

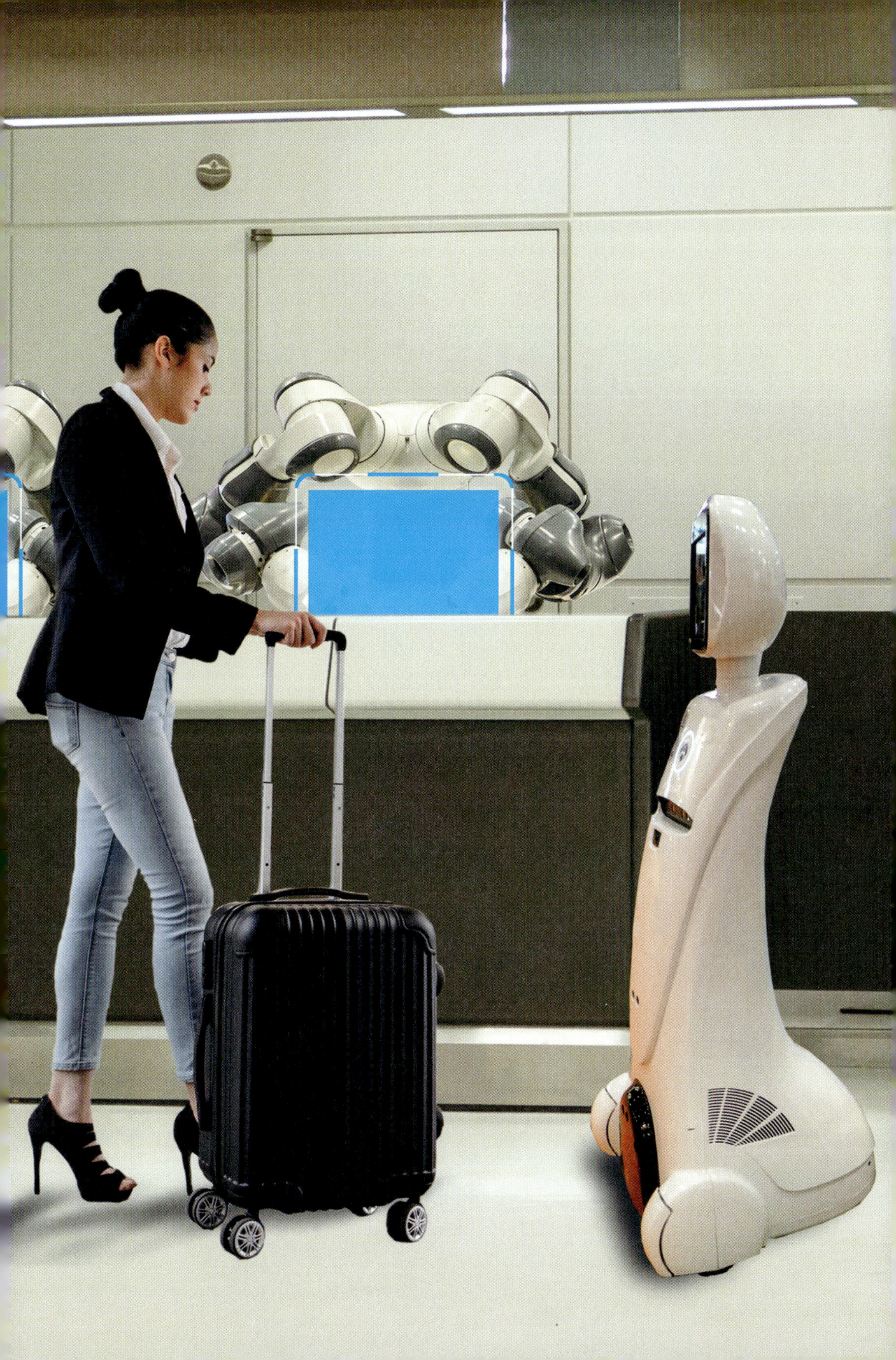

a king-size bed. Your room is 310-B. Your room can be entered by facial recognition. Please stand still while I scan your face."

A moment later, the scan finishes.

"Thank you. Enjoy your stay."

The guest approaches the hotel manager again. "Can I have my luggage brought to my room?" she asks.

"Certainly." The manager calls to a robot. It looks like a luggage rack on wheels. The guest loads her luggage onto the robot. It then makes its way to the elevator.

The guest heads to her room. She passes a vacuum robot in the hallway. She waits until the camera outside her door scans her face.

After a moment, a voice says, "Welcome, Mrs. Adams." The door opens.

Inside, she sees that her bags have been placed inside her closet. A small round robot with large blue eyes sits on the desk. A card next to it has the robot's name. It also explains how to use the robot.

"Alexandria, please set an alarm for 5:00 p.m.," Mrs. Adams says.

Robot vacuum cleaners are already being used to clean hotel hallways and lobbies.

Automation in factories may mean some tasks that once required several workers can be handled by one person.

"Okay, I have set an alarm for 5:00 p.m.," the robot says.

Mrs. Adams takes off her shoes. She lies down on the bed to nap before dinner.

AI AND JOBS OF THE FUTURE

The above example is based on experts' predictions about the future. In the 2010s and early 2020s, new AI technology was added to hotels. This trend will likely continue in the future.

This is just one example of how AI will change the job market. AI will continue to replace repetitive tasks in the workplace. Experts will train AI to do tasks that make work more **efficient**.

CHAPTER ONE

WHAT IS ARTIFICIAL INTELLIGENCE?

Artificial intelligence is the ability of a computer to do tasks usually done by humans. This includes solving problems and learning from experience. AI learns by finding patterns in large amounts of information.

AI still can not do everything that humans can do. However, it has made big leaps forward. Some AI systems can do specific tasks better than humans.

AI improves when it has access to more data. The ability to store more data means AI discovers new patterns and connections.

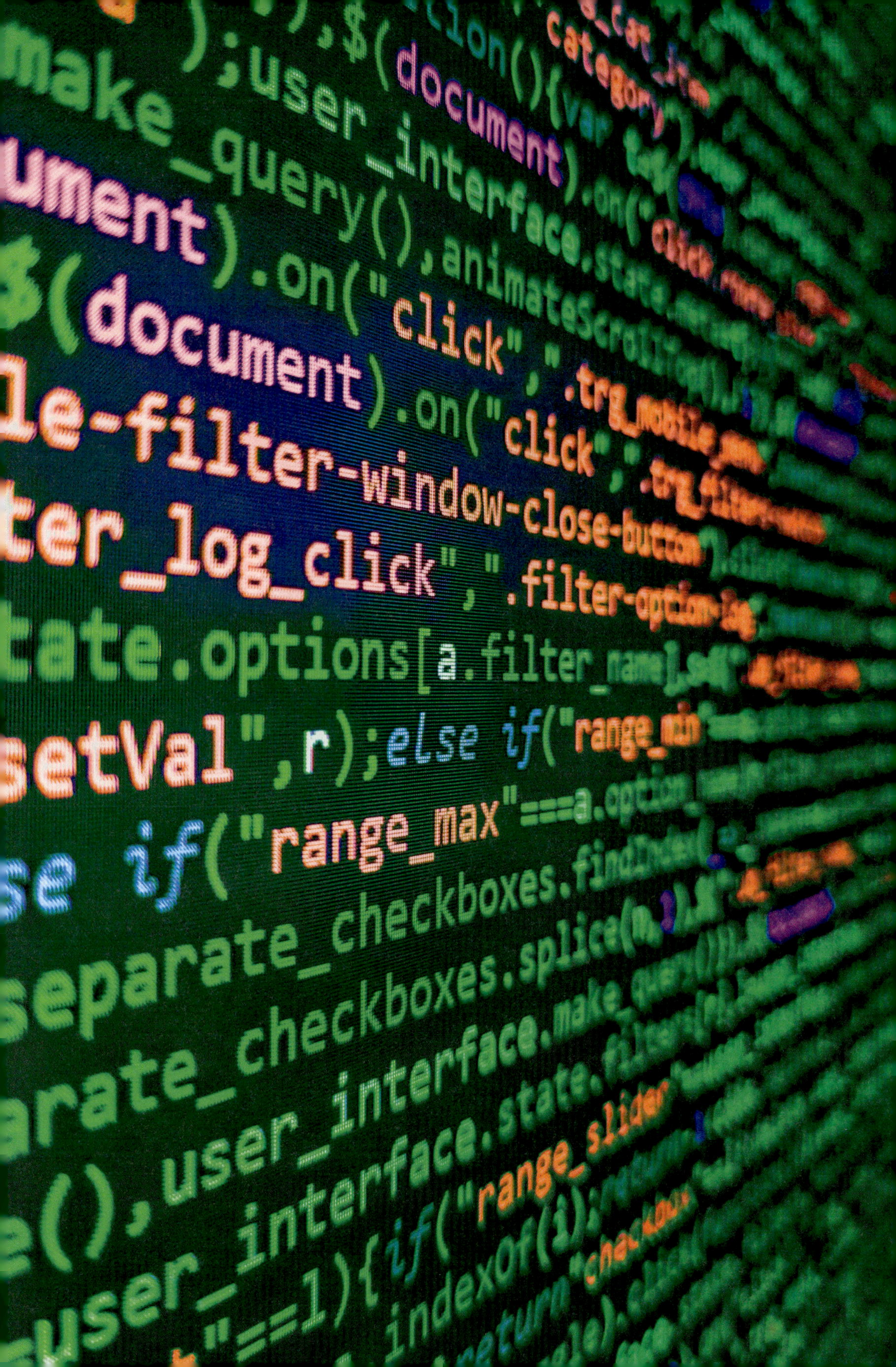

THE BEGINNING OF AI

AI was once just a topic of science fiction. A scientist named Alan Turing changed this. In the 1940s, he had the idea to use computers to solve problems. Turing gave a lecture about artificial intelligence in 1947. He said, "What we want is a machine that can learn from experience."[1]

In 1950, Turing created the Turing Test. Questions would be sent to a subject. The subject might be a computer or a person. If the computer answered the questions as a human would, the computer passed the test. It was believed to be intelligent. This test was designed to see how well AI could imitate humans. But it did not show that a computer could solve problems or reason.

British computer scientist Alan Turing is credited with developing the earliest form of artificial intelligence.

Learning from experience requires a lot of information, or data. Some AI systems gather data. Then they study the patterns in order to create rules. They apply those rules to process new data. This is known as **machine learning**. The more data AI has,

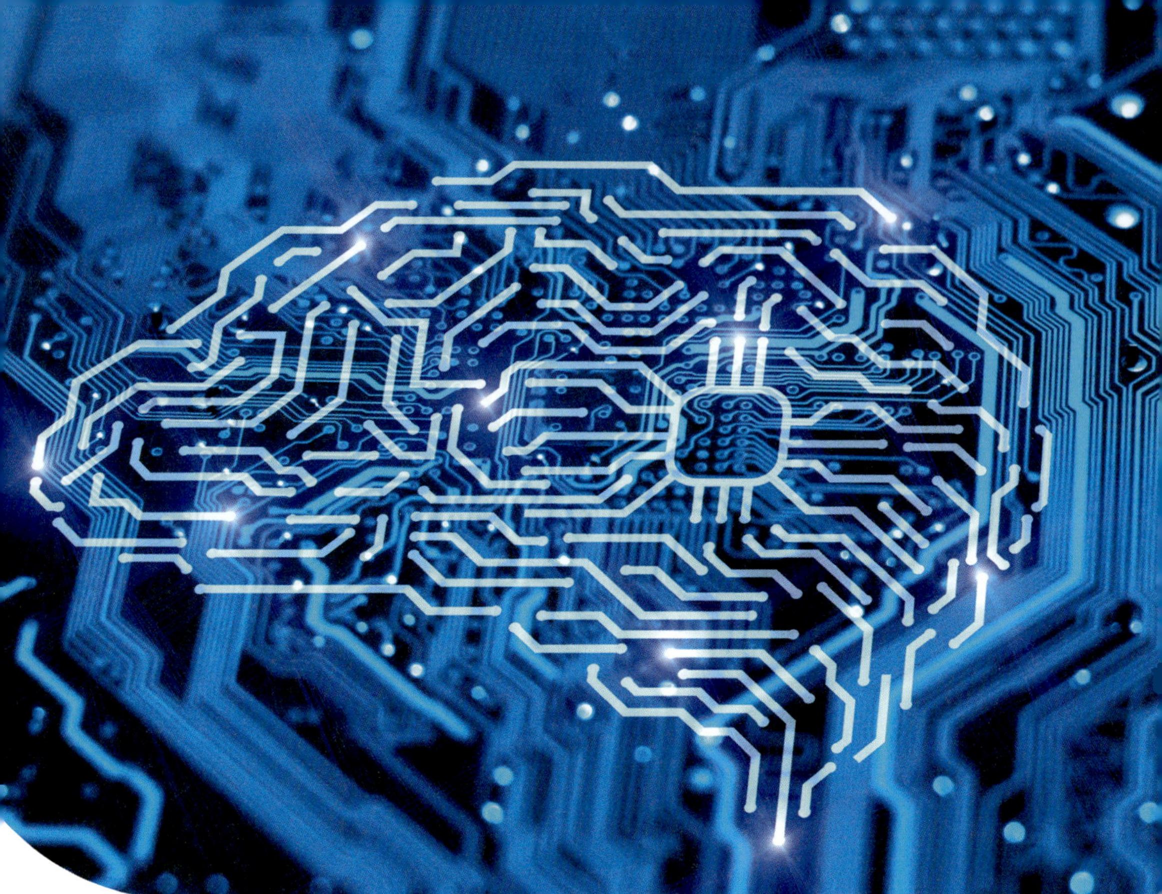

The network that AI develops as it looks for patterns in data has been compared to the neural network of the human brain.

the more patterns it will discover. This is how AI improves.

In 1951, American scientist Marvin Minsky developed one of the first artificial neural networks. These are networks of thousands of **nodes**. These nodes take in and process data. Then they provide data.

The nodes are connected like neurons in a human brain. Different groups of nodes form layers. Each layer looks for different patterns in data. This is a deeper form of machine learning called deep learning. The same basic concept is still used in AI today.

But AI was slow to develop. Computers were not advanced enough yet. They could not process the amount of data needed to power AI. But early forms of AI began to appear in certain jobs, especially in industry.

EARLY JOBS AND AI

The first form of AI used in the workplace was a robot. Robots are autonomous. This means they can work without human help. They can sense their environment and complete tasks. The study of how these machines work is called robotics. Robots often use a simple form of AI to complete their jobs.

Robots can work faster than people. They make fewer mistakes. Since the 1950s, robots have been used in factories. They can do repetitive work. Robots never get tired. They can also work in dangerous places. Robots make work more efficient.

Unimate was the first robot used in a factory. George Devol made this robotic arm in 1961. Unimate was used at a General Motors plant. It helped build cars. Unimate did one basic task. It removed parts from a **press** and stacked them. Workers at the plant didn't like doing this task. So they didn't mind that Unimate took this job. But by the early 1970s, General

Unimate did everything from pouring coffee to helping assemble cars at the General Motors plant.

Motors was using more robots. They did welding. The robots did other tasks on the **assembly line**. Workers lost their jobs. Auto workers went on strike. This is when people refuse to work to get something from their employer. One strike shut down the plant for 22 days.

In 1966, a robot was built at the Stanford Research Institute. It was called Shakey. A user could tell Shakey to do a task. Shakey used sensors to look around. Sensors gather information about the location. They then translate the data into electrical signals. Shakey used these signals to solve problems. This was a simple form of AI.

By 1981, robots were used for more difficult jobs. General Motors used robots that had cameras. They could look at parts and use AI to sort them. Later robots were developed that had vision. They also had machine learning abilities. These robots had many uses in factories and warehouses. Between 1980 and 2020, the number of robots used in the United States grew from about 4,000 to more than 3 million. They have changed workplaces across the country.

Robots and Humans Working Together

In the 2010s, robots and humans began working together. Before this, robots and humans worked separately. This was safer. But adding sensors to robots helped. Robots could sense where humans were. This allowed robots to safely take a part from a person to do a task.

CHAPTER TWO

AI IN THE WORKPLACE

In the early 2020s, AI affected more than just factory jobs. AI technology was being used in cars. Self-driving vehicles began to change transportation.

AI was also used in company warehouses. Marketing was affected by AI. Customer service changed as well. Even jobs such as writing and making music were affected by AI.

Autonomous vehicles are equipped with sensors that help them avoid cars and other obstacles on the road.

VOL
RADIO
MEDIA
MAP
NAV
FRONT
REAR
PASSENGER
AIR BAG
CLIMATE
MODE
DUAL
CleanAir
A/C
TEMP
AUTO
OFF
TEMP

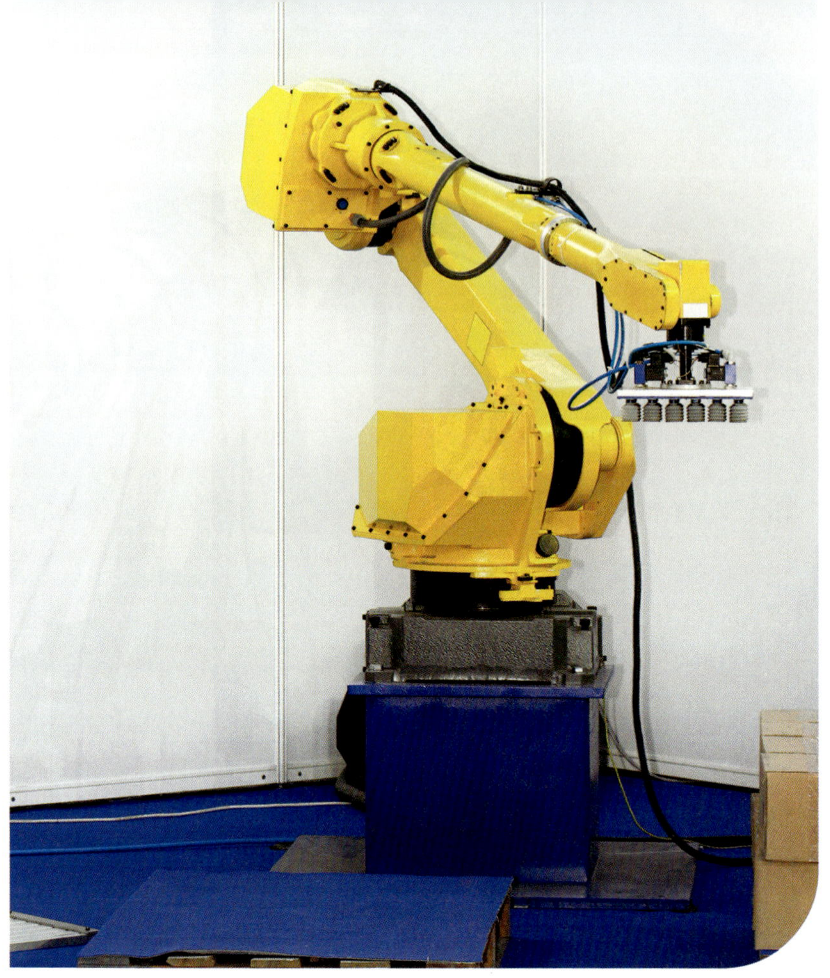

Robotic arms are used in warehouses to pack and move boxes.

AN AUTONOMOUS WORLD

Self-driving taxis were first used in Wuhan, China in 2022. These vehicles are driven by AI instead of humans. The cars use sensors, **algorithms**, and GPS. These tools help safely drive people to

their destinations. One company had
logged more than 1.4 million rides in 2022.

Experts predict millions of jobs may
be lost because of self-driving cars. This
includes jobs such as truck drivers and
parking attendants. But some technical
jobs are expected to grow. People need to
create and fix these vehicles. These jobs will
require new skills.

In 2012, Amazon started using robots in
its warehouses. They carried products from
shelves to pickers and sorters. This saved
the workers a lot of walking. It made
warehouses more productive. At first, the
robots scanned barcodes to find products.
But in 2022, a robot named Sparrow was
created. It found items using cameras
and AI.

An Amazon spokesperson explained how Sparrow improved the work process. They said, "Sparrow will take on repetitive tasks, enabling our employees to focus their time and energy on other things, while also advancing safety."[2] Amazon placed 350,000 AI robots in their warehouses. In the future, robots may replace pickers and sorters in warehouses. Amazon is retraining its workforce. They will shift to more tech-oriented jobs as needed.

GENERATIVE AI AND CREATIVE FIELDS

Generative AI emerged in the 2020s. It uses deep learning to find patterns in data. Prompters are people who train AI systems. They supply AI with lots of data.

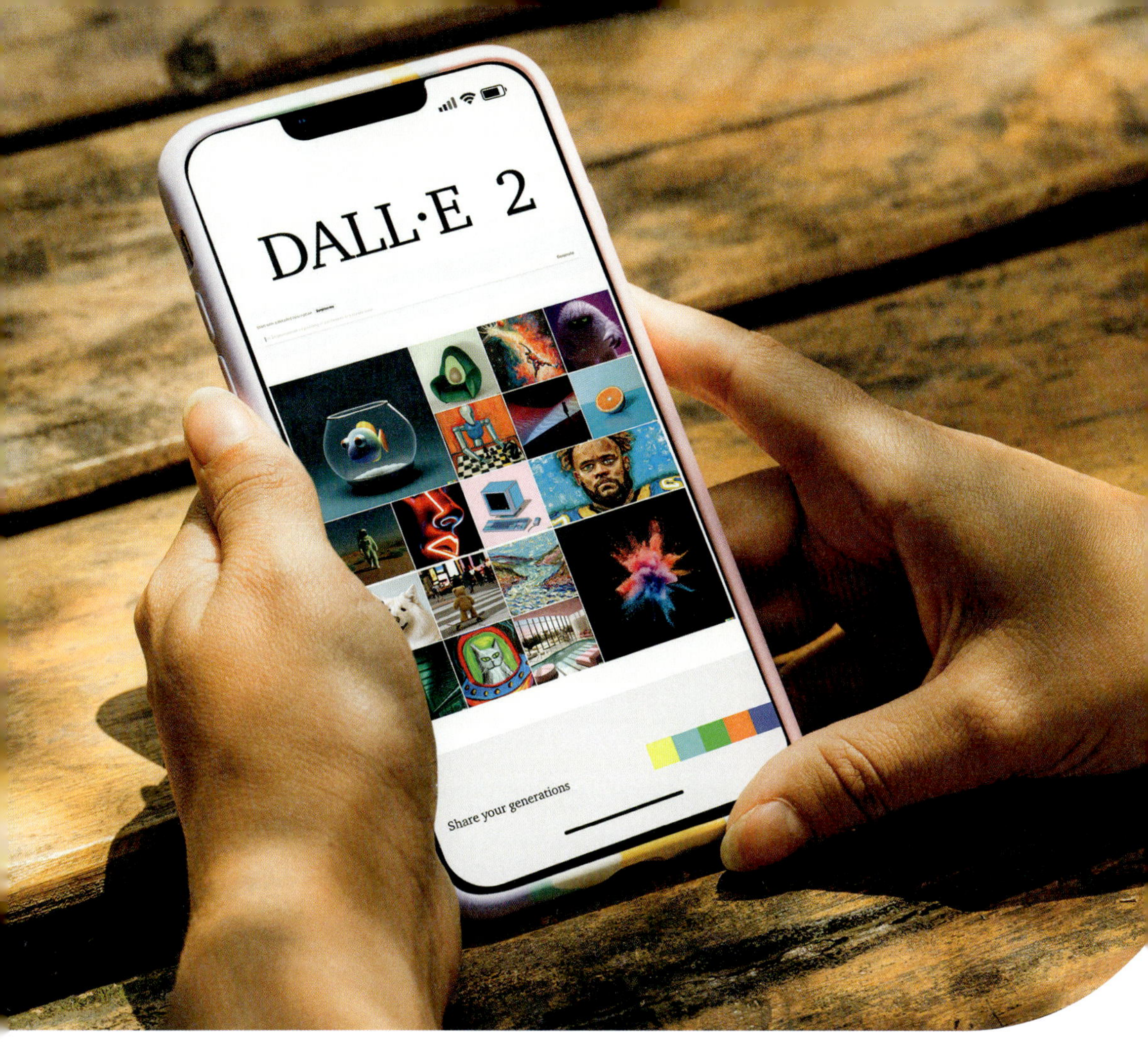

Generative AI tools such as DALL-E and ChatGPT help users create art or text based on data AI finds in existing databases.

They also create algorithms. AI uses these to identify patterns. AI then creates something new based on what it learned. In the early 2020s, the company OpenAI developed two generative AI tools. One of them is called DALL-E. It creates an image based on the text a user types in. The other is ChatGPT. It is a **chatbot**. It can be asked to create any type of text. This includes marketing materials. ChatGPT can also write articles and stories. It can even write computer code.

In 2023, Resume Builder surveyed 1,000 business leaders in the United States.

Chatbots and Jobs

In 2023, the Future of Work Centre at Teesside University in Middlesbrough, England, said chatbot technology was advancing rapidly. The use of AI was increasing in customer service jobs. A 2022 study by Gartner IT predicted that chatbots would be the primary customer service channel for 25 percent of organizations by 2027.

It asked them how they used AI.
Forty-nine percent of companies said they
use ChatGPT. Of those, 48 percent have
replaced workers with AI systems. In the
future, these workers may be required to
know how to use ChatGPT.

Generative AI also affects the music
and video industries. A program called
AudioCraft creates music. AI gathers vast
amounts of music and sounds. With this
software, a user can request a specific type
of music. The program makes music based
on the request.

Vocaloids are programs that mimic
human voices. They are paired with
computer-generated images of performers.
They create a virtual concert experience.
Generative AI allows more people to

enter the music industry. Those without experience can now create their own music. These programs cut costs to produce music. Professional musicians can also use the software to enhance their work. This technology means some jobs may be lost. This includes musicians and producers.

CUSTOMER SERVICE

Many businesses use AI-driven chatbots to talk to customers. For example, Bank of America's website has a chatbot. It provides basic customer service. Current chatbots use **natural language processing**. They use models and examples to help recognize human language. Machine learning helps them learn responses to customer questions.

Vocaloids, such as the digital pop star Hatsune Miku, are popular in Japan.

Many of the repetitive tasks typically done by entry-level office workers could be handled by AI in the future.

Virtual agents are chatbots. They answer basic questions. But some questions are too complicated. This is where human customer service representatives come in. Dr. Mansoor Somro is a sustainability professor in the United Kingdom. He explains that AI won't take over all customer service jobs. "We still appreciate the human interface more," he says.[3]

In the future, AI will continue to affect job markets. It will replace some entry-level and repetitive jobs. But people will still be needed. Those who can adapt will do well. This means using the power of AI to work more efficiently.

CHAPTER THREE

FUTURE OF AI IN THE WORKPLACE

Those in AI development are beginning to think to the future. They are studying new ways AI can be used to improve the way work is done. Experts predict that AI will continue to grow in industries where it is already in use. This includes the health care and law industries. It is also being used to improve education. The way in which AI is used in these fields will shape the future of the job market.

AI's ability to scan multiple databases quickly can help those in the law industry complete time-consuming research.

AI-driven robots can be used to make basic surgical incisions. This allows doctors to focus on the more complicated parts of a surgery.

HEALTH CARE

AI's ability to sort through vast amounts of data is very helpful in health care. It means AI can quickly review medical scans. In one study, AI was able to review hundreds of scans in 90 seconds. It took a team of radiologists 4 hours to review the same amount. AI was also better able to identify small spots in scans than humans. This can help doctors make better decisions about how to treat patients.

AI is also being used in the operating room. Robotic arms can do simple tasks. This might include tying a knot. Then surgeons can focus on the harder parts of a surgery. AI is used to support, not replace, surgeons. Dr. Christopher J. Tignanelli is a surgeon at the University of Minnesota in Minneapolis. He explains, "AI will analyze surgeries as they're being done and potentially provide decision support to surgeons as they're operating."[4]

LAW

In March 2023, an amazing thing happened. An AI program passed the Uniform Bar Exam (UBE). The UBE is an exam lawyers must take to practice law. The AI was created by OpenAI. It was based on the company's ChatGPT product. The AI scored 75 percent on the test. This is higher than 90 percent of humans who take the test.

Experts do not think lawyers will be replaced by AI. But AI may be a powerful tool lawyers can use in the future. AI's deep learning allows AI to search databases quickly. It can look at information from one source and then look through other sources to find supporting evidence. It may also be able to connect text, image, and

With AI completing research, paralegals could focus on meeting with clients or assisting lawyers in the courtroom.

video evidence. AI is fast and efficient. It could allow lawyers to help more people. Using AI will also save their clients money.

Much of this work is currently done by paralegals. They assist lawyers. AI may replace some paralegals. However, paralegals can make AI work for them in the future. This would free up time for them to meet with clients. They could also analyze the work AI produces for them.

SHIPPING AND DELIVERY SERVICES

In the future, AI will be used in autonomous shipping trucks. Trucks with AI are already being tested. Gatik is an autonomous

Big shipping companies such as DHL are experimenting with autonomous trucks for long-haul deliveries.

trucking company. In 2023, it used
about forty-five self-driving trucks to ship
products for companies such as Walmart.
The trucks drove short distances of up to
75 miles (120 km). Richard Steiner is head
of policy and communications for Gatik.
He says, "Over the next few years, you're
definitely going to see autonomous trucks
become increasingly commonplace across
multiple markets."[5] Using them will save
the companies about 30 percent of their
trucking costs. These are the costs to pay
truck drivers, who will no longer be needed.
The trucks can run 24 hours a day.

Trucking companies would like to use
autonomous trucks for long-haul deliveries.
This will make long-haul trucking jobs
a thing of the past. They can switch to

shorter routes. This may allow them to
spend less time away from home. But it will
also reduce truckers' pay. They are paid by
the hour.

Drones will also be a major AI player
in the future. A drone is an aircraft that
does not have a pilot. Most are controlled
remotely. However, autonomous drones are
becoming more common. These drones
can navigate without human help. They can
also see their surroundings. This makes

Digital Doubles

AIs can be used to copy what other people can
do. These types of AI are called digital doubles.
Digital doubles can help a worker by completing
some of their tasks. This helps the worker be
more productive.

drones perfect for delivering goods to places that may be hard to get to. They are faster and more direct than other forms of transportation, too.

With companies using drones for deliveries, people will lose jobs. Delivery drivers will not be needed. But new jobs will also be created. People will be needed to develop, operate, and repair these drones.

EDUCATION

AI will completely change education with the smart classroom. This technology can improve the teaching and learning experience. For example, AI with video recognition can recognize students in the classroom. It can help with attendance. It also studies students' expressions and body language. This information helps teachers see if students are engaged in the lesson.

Intelligent AI programs could offer a more personalized way to teach students. This would allow students to do more basic work with the help of AI. Teachers could use AI to tailor lessons based on students' past performance. Use of AI could free up teachers' time to work more closely with individual students.

The education field may lose jobs due to AI. But AI could allow teachers to get more work done. Sal Kahn is the founder of Khan Academy. He explains how AI will change education. "We're at the cusp of using AI for probably the biggest positive transformation that education has ever

AI learning tools can provide lessons to students who work ahead or need extra help.

seen," he says. "And the way we're going to do that is . . . to give every teacher on the planet an amazing, artificially intelligent teaching assistant."[6]

CHAPTER FOUR

CONCERNS ABOUT AI IN THE WORKPLACE

There are a lot of exciting developments in AI. AI can save companies time and make them more productive. This saves money. But there is also a lot of fear about AI. If AI can do jobs better and faster than human workers, people worry they may no longer be needed. If they are still needed, their roles and pay may be reduced.

People are also concerned about the safety of AI. AI has sometimes made

Robots can improve the safety of human workers by taking on more dangerous jobs, such as welding.

mistakes that have caused harm. And there are **ethical** issues to consider when using AI. For example, AI can be used to copy the work of someone else.

LOSING JOBS TO AI

As AI is used in more industries, people worry about how it will affect jobs. Already AI is being used to do repetitive tasks. These include customer service jobs, delivery of goods, and factory work. In a survey conducted by the Pew Research Center in 2022, 62 percent of Americans believed that AI would have a major impact on workers. About 28 percent said they thought AI would impact their jobs.

Many people are worried about AI in the workplace. In 2023, the Writers Guild of

In May 2023, screenwriters protested the use of AI for writing scripts.

America went on strike against the Alliance of Motion Picture and Television Producers. AI was one of the reasons for the strike. Writers were concerned about movie and

POTENTIAL FOR AI USE IN THE UNITED STATES BY JOB SECTOR

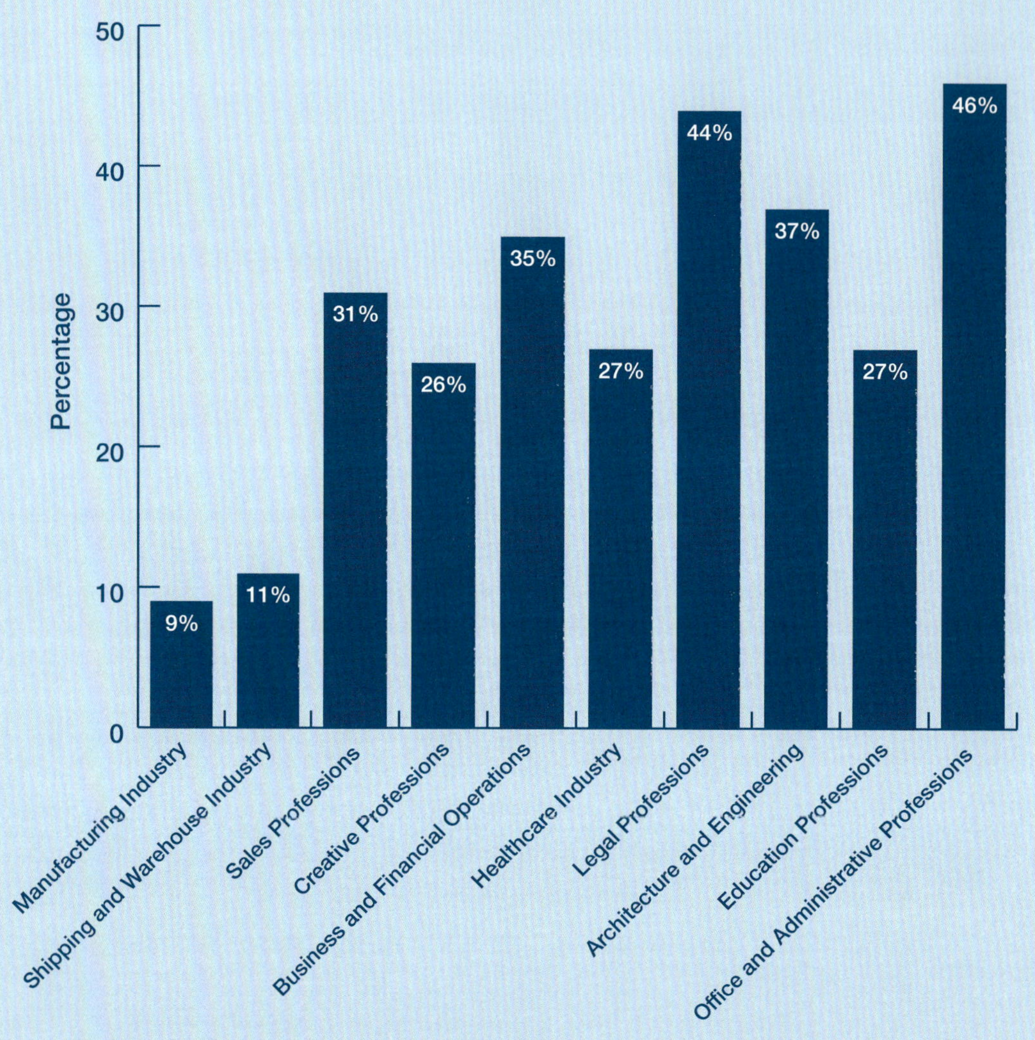

Source: Marcus Lu and Sabrina Lam, "Ranking Industries by Their Potential for AI Automation," Visual Capitalist, June 27, 2023. www.visualcapitalist.com.

With the exception of construction and other manual labor industries, most industries will be affected by AI in the coming years.

television studios using AI to write scripts. This would mean writers would edit scripts instead of writing them. They worried that they would be paid less for this work.

The Screen Actors Guild also went on strike in 2023. Again, AI was one of the reasons. Actors were worried. They thought they could be replaced by AI-generated likenesses in movies and TV shows. Studios may decide to use AI instead of actors. This would lower the studios' costs. Actor Bryan Cranston explains what actors want. "This contract will have a sentence in there that states, 'Actors must be human beings,'" he says. "This is mind-boggling, but that's what it will say, and the same thing with the Writers Guild contract: 'Must be written by a human being.'"[7]

AI AND ERRORS IN THE WORKPLACE

People also fear that AI will make serious mistakes in its work. This has already happened. The AI Incident Database is a record of errors caused by AI. In 2022, 90 incidents occurred. In the first 3 months of 2023, it had already recorded 45 incidents.

Some past incidents were serious. In 2018, Amazon had to stop using AI for job selection. It was ranking women lower than men. This was due to an error in the selection algorithm. Other errors were fatal. In 2018, Lion Air flight 610 was to travel from Jakarta, Indonesia, to the island of Sumatra. Bad data from a sensor caused the plane's AI system to take over and dive into the

Java Sea. The crash killed all 189 people on board.

Companies using AI can avoid mistakes. This means taking the time to learn how to use AI safely. Those using AI should know exactly what AI can do. Someone should always watch over AI to make sure it is operating as it should. Training AI with accurate data will help avoid mistakes. AI should also be trained on data that is

Lion Airlines passengers lost their lives due to an AI error in 2018.

not biased. Finally, AI should be thoroughly tested before it is used in business.

AI AND ETHICS

There are many ethical issues related to the use of AI. Publishers have concerns. They worry that authors will use AI to write books. This content may have biases or false information. This would cause legal problems for the publisher. Authors are

Unilever is one of many companies that has come up with boundaries and a plan for safer use of AI.

worried as well. They fear their work may
be used to feed AI's algorithms without
permission. People in creative fields fear
they may be replaced by AI. They worry
their rights to be paid for their work won't
be honored.

AI has the potential to create unsafe
conditions or misuse private data. To avoid
this, businesses must set rules before
they begin to use AI technology. Unilever
has created its own AI policies. One
states that any decision that significantly
affects someone's life should not be fully
automated. Businesses must also set up
a way to monitor AI technology. This is the
only way to make sure rules are followed.

Laws must be passed to protect people
from AI dangers. President Joe Biden

proposed an AI Bill of Rights in 2022. It would address five key areas. AI should be safe. It should not discriminate. It should protect people's privacy. AI should be clear about what it does. And there should be a way to opt out of using AI.

AI'S CONTINUED EFFECT ON THE JOB MARKET

Despite all the fears people have about AI and the job market, two things are clear. First, AI is not going away. It has been growing at an incredible rate since ChatGPT was introduced in November 2022. AI will keep growing. Second, AI will continue to have a big effect on the job market.

There are many advantages to using AI in different fields. Demis Hassabis is the founder of DeepMind, a technology company. He says, "The future of work lies in the collaboration between humans and AI, where technology enhances our natural abilities . . . empowering us to drive innovation in the workplace."[8] With laws, people, and tools in place to keep AI in check, it can bring many benefits to the workplace.

AI and People Working Together

At the consulting firm Deloitte, employees are using AI successfully. AI tools read over 1.5 million social media comments. They gather feedback on grocery stores. Then they group comments into categories. AI studies the data and helps resolve customers' concerns.

GLOSSARY

algorithms

sets of rules used to solve problems

assembly line

a line of workers in a factory where each worker does one part of a redundant job

chatbot

AI that creates responses based on user prompts

efficient

completing more tasks with less effort

ethical

being truthful, fair, and honest

machine learning

AI that allows systems to learn and improve from experience

natural language processing

the capability of an AI to understand human language

nodes

electronic devices attached to a network

press

a machine that shapes metal

SOURCE NOTES

CHAPTER ONE: WHAT IS ARTIFICIAL INTELLIGENCE?

1. Quoted in B.J. Copeland, "Alan Turing and the Beginning of AI," *Encyclopædia Britannica*, n.d. www.britannica.com.

CHAPTER TWO: AI IN THE WORKPLACE

2. Quoted in Marcus Law, "Amazon Warehouse Robot Uses AI to Handle Millions of Items," *Technology Magazine*, November 15, 2022. www.technologymagazine.com.

3. Quoted in Giulia Carbonaro, "AI Is 'Absolutely' Coming After Your Job If You Work in Customer Service. But It's Not All Bad," *Euronews Next*, October 10, 2023. www.euronews.com.

CHAPTER THREE: FUTURE AI IN THE WORKPLACE

4. Quoted in Jim McCartney, "AI Is Poised to 'Revolutionize' Surgery," *American College of Surgeons Bulletin*, June 7, 2023. www.facs.org.

5. Quoted in Patrick Seitz, "Autonomous Trucks Are Barreling Ahead, but Robot Big Rigs Face a Bumpy Road," *Investor's Business Daily*, March 1, 2023. www.investors.com.

6. Quoted in Vicki Phillips, "Intelligent Classrooms: What AI Means for the Future of Education," *Forbes*, June 7, 2023. www.forbes.com.

CHAPTER FOUR: CONCERNS ABOUT AI IN THE WORKPLACE

7. Quoted in Amanda Harding, "'Breaking Bad' Cast Reunites on Picket Line, Slams AI: 'Dehumanizing the Workforce,'" *Daily Wire*, August 30, 2023. www.dailywire.com.

8. Quoted in Fergal O'Shea, "24 Insightful Quotes from AI Industry Leaders," *Aiifi*, April 8, 2023. www.aiifi.ai.

FOR FURTHER RESEARCH

BOOKS

Jennifer Kaul, *The Potential of Artificial Intelligence*. San Diego, CA: BrightPoint Press, 2025.

Pamela McCauley, *Engineering for Teens*. New York: Rockridge Press, 2021.

Dr. Claire Quigley, *Simply Artificial Intelligence*. New York: DK, 2023.

INTERNET SOURCES

"AI and You: AI Guide for Teens," *UNICEF Office of Global Insight and Policy*, November 2021. www.unicef.org.

"What is AI?" *IBM*, n.d. www.ibm.com.

"Training Machines Together," *National Geographic*, March 21, 2024. www.cducation.natonalgeographic.org.

WEBSITES

OpenAI
www.openai.com

OpenAI is the company that developed ChatGPT. Its website explains the uses for OpenAI products and provides information about types of AI. The site also includes articles about OpenAI research.

Teens in AI
www.teensinai.com

Teens in AI is a website that encourages teens to get involved and share ideas and insights on AI topics. It offers courses and workshops to educate teens on AI topics. It also offers teens the chance to work together to solve real-world problems using AI.

The Youth AI Lab
www.youthai.org

The Youth AI Lab is a website that makes machine learning concepts more accessible to teens. Teens learn through peer-to-peer mentoring opportunities and by hearing from AI experts in the field. They can connect with others to work on meaningful projects related to AI.

INDEX

algorithms, 24, 27, 52, 55
Amazon, 25–26, 52
autonomous vehicles, 22, 24–25, 40–41

biases, 54–55
Biden, Joe, 56

chatbots, 28, 30, 33
ChatGPT, 28–29, 38, 56
Cranston, Bryan, 51–52
customer service, 22, 28, 30–33, 48, 57

DALL-E, 28
deep learning, 17, 26–27, 38
Devol, George, 18
drones, 42–43

education, 34, 43–45, 50
ethical issues, 48, 54–56

facial recognition, 8

General Motors, 18–21
generative AI, 26–30

Hassabis, Demis, 57
health care, 34, 36–37

job loss, 41, 44, 48–52

Khan, Sal, 44–45

law, 34, 38–40

machine learning, 15–17, 20–21, 30–33
Minsky, Marvin, 17

OpenAI, 27–28, 38

robotic arms, 18, 37
robots, 8–10, 18–21, 25–26

safety, 21, 24–25, 26, 46–48, 53, 55–56
self-driving vehicles, 22, 24–25, 40–41
sensors, 20, 21, 24, 53
Shakey, 20
Somro, Mansoor, 33
Sparrow, 25–26
Steiner, Richard, 41

Tignanelli, Christopher, 37
truck drivers, 25, 41–42
Turing, Alan, 14

Unimate, 18–20

vocaloids, 29–30

Writers Guild of America, 49–51

IMAGE CREDITS

ABOUT THE AUTHOR

George Anthony Kulz is a member of the Society of Children's Book Writers and Illustrators and has taken courses at the Institute of Children's Literature and the Gotham Writers' Workshop. He writes for young people and adults.